AF413131

THE 3 P'S

KEEP PRESSING!
KEEP PRAISING!
& KEEP PRAYING!

INSPIRING YOU TO PRESS FORWARD, BY FAITH.

Minister Bernard Marrow

ByFaithWeGood
"For We Walk By Faith, Not By Sight"
2 Corinthians 5:7 KJV

BFWG Ministry Inc.

TABLE OF CONTENTS

ACKNOWLEDGMENTS

First, giving honor to God who is truly the head of my life. Who is my all in all! God has been with me every step of the way. Without Him, I am nothing.

I thank God for my wife Vanessa who supports me 100%! And for my family, my mom, sisters, nieces, and nephews who are the inspiration that help keep me focused.

ABOUT THIS BOOK

The 3 P's was given to me by God and is structured to help you be consistent in pressing forward by faith. God created us to give Him praise and to always succeed, to live a victorious abundant life. However, because of our feelings, worries, distractions, difficult circumstances and seasons, and fear, we find ourselves holding back. We try to press forward in uncertainty instead of full assurance that God is always with us and He'll always have us covered. God has given me The 3 P's to share with you all to help you press forward by faith, by any means necessary.

Keep Pressing! Keep Praising! Keep Praying!

A WORD FROM
THE AUTHOR

All of us have had times in our lives, where we wonder or try to figure out how to move forward from where we are. We try to figure out how to overcome the obstacles and press through the challenges that come our way. Why does it seem so hard for situations to change and for us to experience what God promised?

Can I tell you why, Family? It's our lack of consistency and focus. We allow our feelings to get in the way too much! We get caught up with focusing on others around us, how they live and what they have. We measure ourselves according to what we see on social media when we are created to be uniquely who God created us to be.

With this book, we're going to learn how to press forward the right way.

Philippians 3:13-14 King James Version
"Brethren, I count not myself to have apprehended: but this one thing I do, forgetting those things which are behind, and reaching forth unto those things which are before, I press toward the mark for the prize of the high calling of God in Christ Jesus."

We're created to go confidently in the direction God is leading us. Remember, God doesn't want us looking to the past but moving on, staying focused, letting nothing and no one interfere. We must be united with the Lord! Walking by faith is never giving up on your dreams, the vision, and purpose God has assigned to you to fulfill. It is believing without a doubt that God has a greater plan for your life.

So, "be ye stedfast, unmoveable, always abounding in the work of the Lord" (1 Corinthians 15:58 KJV). Let the Lord lead you. Believe without a doubt that God has a greater plan for your life. Get ready and get in position.

Yes, it takes courage. It can be hard sometimes, but Keep Pressing! Keep Praising! & Keep Praying!

With this book, Family, you'll learn how to do just that.

CHAPTER 1

KEEP PRESSING!

Keep Pressing Towards God

Luke 18:1 New Living Translation
"One day Jesus told his disciples a story to show that they should always pray and never give up."

In Luke 18, Jesus tells the parable of the persistent widow. She was a woman on her own in life, certainly marginalized as an elderly woman. She came to a judge that was not considered righteous, who neither feared God nor cared about people, to ask for justice against her adversary. The judge refused her the justice she sought, but time and time again she came with her request. It was because of her persistence that the judge finally granted her justice.

God honors consistency. Being consistent in tough times is what gets us the results we desire and pray for. We have to be consistent in the way we press forward. There are times when pressing forward doesn't seem easy. There are many obstacles and challenges that come our way. But I want you to know, Family, that God has created and equipped us to press past any and every situation.

God created and equipped us to persevere. Perseverance is a powerful force. It is the one virtue that multiplies the value of who you are and what you do. Love, goodness, kindness, integrity, and your productivity all become worthless if not maintained through perseverance. Perseverance is key when it comes to pressing forward and being consistent in the way you press forward. The best-laid plans, to-do lists, and goals are just dreams without perseverance and motivation. Goal-setting and planning are your roadmaps to success, but perseverance is what pushes you forward toward the ultimate goal and accomplishments.

Pressing forward toward God and the purpose He assigned to your life to fulfill is learning how to persevere and be determined. You have to have a made-up mind, knowing and taking ownership of the direction God is leading you. You must be determined to not allow anyone or anything to get in your way or hold you back. To keep pressing forward is to know your value, your worth, who you are, and whose you are. You are a child of the Most High God, saved by Jesus! You have no limitations. You are loved, protected, covered, cared for and taken care of. You are guaranteed victory through Jesus Christ.

To keep pressing forward is to be focused and determined, to never give up, to never quit. You've seen how God has been with you. You've seen what He worked out in your life before. You have evidence that God is so real and so alive! You've had plenty of moments where you've experienced "the goodness of the LORD in the land of the living" (Psalm 27:13 KJV). That's enough to be determined to continue to keep pressing by any means necessary.

2 Corinthians 4:8-9 KJV
"We are troubled on every side, yet not distressed; we are perplexed, but not in despair; Persecuted, but not forsaken; cast down, but not destroyed."

These verses are such a great description of our relationship with Jesus Christ. It is not easy, but we are never defeated! In life, there will be times when you will go through tough seasons. It's in these moments that you must lean on God more than ever.

The press is vital to our walk because it keeps us humble by consistently reminding us of what Jesus went through for us. It consistently reminds us that our feelings can't get in the way of God's plan for His glory and our lives. It consistently keeps us in a place of growth. Most importantly, the press reminds us that He lives in us. When we are pressed, Jesus is always revealed. The press can be challenging because we can't see the finish line, but God is the author of our story. Even though we don't like the press, the process, and what God has allowed to take place in our lives, we must understand, Family, that God allows hard times to press us forward.

You may be knocked down at times, but you're never knocked out. With God, we always win!

We have to be mindful as we press forward. We all have had moments when we were mad without knowing why. We were blinded to how the situation could be handled better. Otherwise we would have asked ourselves why we are mad in the first place. This is one of the ways the enemy will try to come against you. The enemy knows who he can and can't touch and come at. He knows he has nothing unless you give him power or access to you.

This is why we need to remain strong in faith as we press forward and not get caught up in our feelings. When you're in your feelings, you're not in faith. If you're not in faith, you're not covered. But with God, you'll always win, in Jesus' Name. We keep pressing toward God, because we can't lose with Him. We keep pressing towards God, because His way is always the best way. We stay focused and keep pressing towards God, because it's our responsibility too. We keep pressing towards God, because He's the author and finisher of our faith.

Hebrews 12:2 KJV
"Looking unto Jesus the author and finisher of our faith; who for the joy that was set before him endured the cross, despising the shame, and is set down at the right hand of the throne of God."

Pressing forward is a mindset. We must have the mindset of choosing to declare, "I'm focused! I will follow Jesus." We need to learn and always remember when it comes to pressing forward is to stay focused and look to Jesus. I've shared this with many people before. Renewing your mind and staying focused is knowing to go to God. That is the first order of business. Our relationship with Jesus Christ and His Word is our foundation. He is a foundation that will never be shaken.

Let's stay right here for a while. We can learn a lot about the importance of pressing forward and keeping our eyes fixed on Jesus by going deeper into Hebrews 12:2. In Hebrews 12, we see the result of persevering, obedient faith in Christ. The race set before the Hebrews, wherein they must either win the crown of glory or have everlasting misery for their portion, is the same race set before us.

We must understand the sin to which we are most prone or to

which we are most exposed by habit, age, or circumstances—that sin that does so easily beset us. This is an important exhortation, for if a person's darling sin—be it what it will—remains unsubdued, it will hinder many from running the Christian race (pressing forward). It takes from them every motive for running the race set before them, hindering them from pressing forward, and gives power to every discouragement.

Hebrews 12 is one of the great moving passages of the New Testament. In it, the writer gives us a summary of the Christian life in the importance of pressing forward and staying focused while having a personal relationship with Jesus Christ.

This chapter of Hebrews also makes it abundantly clear that we are not alone. Not only are there a multitude of folks who have gone before us and passed faith on to us, there are also a multitude of folks who are running the race with us right now. We are in position to keep pressing together. We are saints, God's children. Saints are the believers. Saints are the redeemed. Saints make up the Church of Jesus Christ.

Saints are people in position to set examples for other believers and for nonbelievers. We know who God created us to be, but we also know our sins and shortcomings. We know what holds us back, causes distractions, puts us in our feelings, and causes roadblocks. These things can cause us to feel less-than, unworthy, or not good enough. But we are enough! We are created by God to press forward continually and victoriously.

We all have times in our lives when we are distracted by the world, caught up in the decisions we made, the habits we had, and the places and people we hung around. We still have moments when temptation comes, but we must remember we are all sinners saved by grace through faith. Grace is a free gift from God. There is nothing we can do or have done to earn it or deserve it. It is given to us by the One who loves us more than any of us could possibly imagine. It is given to us by the One who has gone before us, marked out the race for us, the pioneer and perfecter, "the author and finisher of our faith" (Hebrews 12:2 KJV): Jesus Christ.

The writer of Hebrews uses the idea of a race as a way to explain the Christian journey. It is a metaphor. I think we get it wrong if we interpret this metaphor to mean that we are running as fast as we can in order to get this life over with or win a prize. The Christian life is not a sad or sadistic life. It is a life to be lived by faith abundantly. While most runners are joyful only at the end of a race, we are to find joy in running the race itself—at the beginning, middle, and end. We can do this because we already have the prize. The prize has been won by the "perfecter, the author and finisher of our faith," once and for all. Jesus Christ went to the cross and died for our sins and is now alive forevermore. Because of this, we can boldly move forward, continually pressing forward in serving God and our neighbors in love, passing on the faith that has been passed on to us.

In this race we are running there are no losers and there is no competition. Instead we are all running it together as God's children. Some run alongside us and some run in front of us to help us along the way. Up ahead is Jesus in first place, giving us the will, ability, and strength to run, to keep pressing, and showing us the way the race goes. This is why we are to fix our eyes upon Him. With our eyes fixed on Jesus, we can stay focused and keep pressing, pressing toward God and fulfilling the purpose He assigned to our life.

No matter what, you've got to keep pressing, Family! Press forward by faith. Remember when Jesus was approached by Nicodemus? This great teacher of Israel asked how to enter the Kingdom of God and inherit eternal life. Jesus said, "You must be born again" (John 3:1-21). Even Jesus' instruction to His disciples was, "Follow me" (Matthew 16:24).

God is saying to you, Family, to throw away the junk that you are caught up in or that has you caught up—the bad habits, what you think is the right path to take, the lifestyle you live—and "Follow me." This is what Christ is saying to us: "Follow me."

There are times when the journey becomes joyless and it is difficult to focus on pressing forward. This occurs when we take our eyes off Jesus by giving in to opposition and temptation, such as believing the world when it tries to sell us a bill of rotten goods. When we follow the world's system, instead of living according to the Word of God, we grow weary and lose heart. When things aren't going our way or when we feel sick, we depend on those in the world instead of Jesus, the Creator of the world. In these moments, we are focused on our problems and not our purpose.

Psalm 30:4-6 KJV

"Sing unto the Lord, O ye saints of his, and give thanks at the remembrance of his holiness. For his anger endureth but a moment; in his favour is life: weeping may endure for a night, but joy cometh in the morning. And in my prosperity I said, I shall never be moved."

David's faith in God advanced to an unshaken steadfastness: his confidence and joy in God were strong and complete. Just like David, you can have strong faith in God knowing He'll always come through for you. God will take care of your problems; just take care of the assignment He's given you!

There may come issues or situations that aren't easy to deal with. You may become distracted, focusing on your problems and not your purpose. Family, you must keep your eyes on Jesus. That way you'll praise God for who He is anyhow, and you'll keep pressing forward toward God anyway! Life may seem hard sometimes, but joy will always come in the morning! "The joy of the LORD is your strength" (Nehemiah 8:10 KJV)! In our prosperity, we shall never be moved. We are always victorious when we keep our eyes on Jesus.

When you take your eyes off Jesus:

- You lose out.
- You're unfocused.
- You become distracted and can get caught up under the influence and the power of Satan.
- You'll find yourself always trying to handle situations on your own.
- You'll find yourself being in the wrong places at the wrong times.

When you take your eyes off Jesus and don't remain prayerful, studying God's Word, you can become uncovered. The Lord instructed me to write this book to encourage you to make up your mind and declare by faith right now that you're gonna keep pressing. It is time to declare, "I'm focused and I will follow Jesus!"

What happens to people when they look anywhere but to God? Family, there is a great difference between what happens when we take our eyes off of God and what God can do through us when we stay focused on Him. God gave me some examples in the Bible to share with you.

- Adam and Eve: What happened when they took their eyes off God and on to a fruit? They sinned.
- Cain: What happened when he took his eyes off of God and on to his brother? He killed Abel.
- The world: What happened to mankind when they took their eyes off of God and on to their own selfish desires? The flood came and everyone died except those in the ark.
- Lot's wife: What happened when she took her eyes off of God and looked back to see Sodom? She became a pillar of salt.
- Moses: What happened to him when he took his eyes off God and tried to help the Israelites his own way? He killed an Egyptian.
- The Israelites: What happened to them when they took their eyes off of God and on to their circumstances? They wandered in the wilderness for forty years.
- Samson: What happened to him when he took his eyes off of God and on to a woman? He was tricked by Delilah and captured by the Philistines.
- Saul: What happened to him when he took his eyes off of God and on to doing his own will? He was rejected as king.
- David: What happened to him when he took his eyes off of God and on to Bathsheba? His son died and he almost lost his kingdom.
- The Disciples: What happened when they took their eyes off of God and on to their circumstances? They denied and abandoned Jesus.

But wait a minute. What happens to people in God's Word when they fix their eyes on Jesus?

- Noah's family was saved.

- Abel now lives with God forever.
- Abraham became the father of a great and numerous nation.
- Joseph became a mighty man in Egypt and helped his family.
- Moses led the children of Israel out of Egypt.
- Samson regained his strength and killed the Philistines.
- David became king and defeated his enemies.
- The Disciples took the gospel to the world.
- Steven saw the Glory of God.
- Paul preached the gospel in prison and out of prison.

When you keep your eyes on Jesus, you'll walk in your purpose. You'll never miss out on a move of God because you will always be in position for God to work miracles in your life and in those around you. When you keep your eyes on Jesus, you can walk in the guaranteed victory that He's given you. When you keep your eyes on Jesus, you can "walk by faith, not by sight" (2 Corinthians 5:7 KJV)!

Family, make up in your mind and declare today and every day of your life: "I'm going to keep pressing. Pressing forward by faith. Pressing toward God. I'm Focused on following Jesus!"

Proverbs 14:12 reminds us that "there is a way that seems right to a man, but its end is the way of death" (New King James Version).

Many of us are taught to view life as some kind of a pyramid with those on the bottom serving those above them. We often envy the people at the top, thinking joy and happiness is found in being served. Some passionately seek to be at the top of the world's imaginary pyramid. They reach desperately for the money, fame, or power that they think will put them higher in the eyes of the world. Some think this is what this life is all about. But all this is a lie.

When you fix your eyes on Jesus and follow Him, you'll find that life is actually more fulfilling. When we intentionally choose to be like Jesus, He makes us an example of faith, even helping others. Walking by faith and helping others pushes us forward in the right direction, giving us the right desire to keep pressing. In helping others, we find great freedom. We take the focus off of ourselves and put all the focus on Jesus. Thus we live our lives by faith with less stress, less anxiety, and less frustration. We begin to feel more fulfilled, more complete, and more alive, pressing forward by faith freely. Living for God and others completely abolishes our need for a pecking order. A great weight is lifted off our shoulders when we no longer seek power and mastery over others. When we no longer seek to make everything about ourselves, but instead make it all about Jesus, it becomes easier to keep pressing, pressing toward God in the right direction that He's leading us.

Having real joy and the desire to keep pressing are found not in having attention and being served but in choosing to focus on Jesus and serve others.

As we keep pressing forward, let's "throw off everything that hinders and the sin that so easily entangles…[Let's run and keep pressing] with perseverance the race marked out for us, fixing our eyes on Jesus, the pioneer and perfecter of faith. For the joy set before him, he endured the cross, scorning its shame, and sat down at the right hand of the throne of God. [Let us] consider him who endured such opposition from sinners, so that [we] will not grow weary and lose heart" (Hebrews 12:1-3 New International Version) but keep pressing forward by faith. In doing so, we will not only discover great joy in the race, being equipped to keep pressing forward by faith, but we will also be people that the light of God shines through. As we lift up the Name of Jesus, He'll draw all men unto Himself (John 12:32).

Family, it's truly a joy to be consistent in pressing forward. When you can recognize how God is moving in your life, how He's been with you every step of the way, you are inspired to keep going. God has brought you this far; be encouraged and know that He wants to take you further.

I want to share three more great scriptures with you that will also inspire you to keep pressing, keep pressing toward God.

Isaiah 43:18-19 KJV
"Remember ye not the former things, neither consider the things of old. Behold, I will do a new thing; now it shall spring forth; shall ye not know it? I will even make a way in the wilderness, and rivers in the desert."

As you continue to keep pressing, you're pressing away from the old and stepping into the new! You can decree and declare that every day moving forward shall be the best day of your life in Jesus' Mighty Name. Speak over yourself. Speak over your year. Speak over your job. Speak over the goals you set. Speak over your family. Declare you will overcome every obstacle, that every situation will work for your good, that you will prosper, that you will live and declare the works of the Lord (Psalm 118:17). Speak it, believe it, and receive it in Jesus' Mighty Name!

Jesus did everything by faith. Every area of our life is to be lived by faith. We've got the victory through Jesus Christ, and there's nothing the enemy can do about it!

Psalms 32:8 NLT
"The Lord says, 'I will guide you along the best pathway for your life. I will advise you and watch over you.'"

The things we come up against and deal with in life are not always easy. Even with conviction and good decisions, certain people, places, and things may not always be easy to let go of. But with God all things are possible.

Pressing forward each day is an opportunity for God to have His way in your life as you seek Him. God loves it when we seek Him daily for change in our lives. When we make ourselves available to Him, He'll begin to transform and prepare us for our next level in Him. Step by step, day by day, you will get better at letting go of anything that is a distraction, hindrance, or bad for you, your health, and your family. God is always with you, ready to help, love, and forgive you.

This is why you must keep pressing. With God, you're secure. He's leading you and watching over you at all times. You will never lose when you follow God's directions and press forward in the way He's guiding you.

Proverbs 4:25-27 NLT
"Look straight ahead, and fix your eyes on what lies before you. Mark out a straight path for your feet; stay on the safe path. Don't get sidetracked; keep your feet from following evil."

These are God's instructions concerning how we press forward faithfully. Stay focused on God's Word. Focus on where God is taking you. Focus on the life He's created for you. Focus on the blessings He has in store for you. Focus on the healing He's already done and promised He will do in you. Focus on God's joy; that is our strength. Focus on the promises He will fulfill through and for you. Focus on the family He's created you to love. Focus on God's love that's freely available to you. Focus on how He is a very present help.

Look ahead at all the moments you will share, giving God the glory for all He's done! God has more before you than behind you. Don't let the distractions of this world keep you from focusing on God and the plan and purpose He has for you. Never let anyone or anything stop you from pressing forward. Situations may be hard and challenging sometimes, but with God you'll never lose. You'll never fail. You will always win!

Keep Pressing, Family. Keep pressing toward God. He has you covered, and there's nothing any man or the enemy can do about it. Let the Lord lead you!

#ByFaithWeGood

CHAPTER 2
KEEP PRAISING!
Keep Praising His Holy Name

Psalms 150:1-6 KJV
"Praise ye the LORD. Praise God is his sanctuary: praise him in the firmament of his power. Praise him for his mighty acts: praise him according to his excellent greatness. Praise him with the sound of the trumpet: praise him with the psaltery and harp. Praise him with the timbrel and dance: praise him with stringed instruments and organs. Praise him upon the loud cymbals: praise him upon the high sounding cymbals. Let everything that hath breath praise the LORD. Praise ye the LORD."

Praise must be a priority in our lives.

Why is it so important to praise God? Why is it important to worship God? What does it accomplish for us?

Do you know who is the greatest saint in the world? It is not he or she who prays the most or fasts the most; it is not he or she who gives the most alms, or is most eminent in temperance, chastity, or justice. It is he or she who is always thankful to God, who wills everything that God willeth, who receives everything as an instance of God's goodness and has a heart always ready to praise God for it.

The praise and worship we offer reveals our love for God and our thankfulness for who He is and all that He's done. It is an essential aspect of being a Christian. As children of God, we offer our praise, love, and life to God. Praise and worship is not just an act or expression that happens in church on Sunday mornings. It is a lifestyle that drives us to desire to become more like Jesus.

Giving God praise is what we should do every day, all day! Giving God praise ought to be a part of our everyday lives. Regardless of what is going on in our lives, we should not let anything or anybody separate or steal the joy we have in Jesus. We serve a mighty

God! Because of who God is and how good He's been, we should always give Him a mighty praise.

Remember, Family, God honors consistency. In spite of hard times, we keep praising God, because "God inhabits the praises of His people" (Psalms 22:3). We keep praising God, because by faith our praise to Him grants us access to who God is and all that He has promised.

When you keep praising God's Holy Name you don't have to worry over what you need. You just praise God for who He is because, if you have faith, it's happening. What you need is becoming available and God is working out every situation for your good. When you press forward by faith, remain consistent, and keep praising God, everything weighing you down now is lifted!

Let's go deeper.

PRAISE = *to commend, to applaud or magnify.*

For believers, children of God, praise to God is an expression of worship, lifting up, and glorifying the Lord.

WORSHIP = *to ascribe worth, to pay homage, to revere.*

We have been called to lift up the name of Jesus, to humble ourselves and adore Him. The problem is that we try to praise and worship God with other concerns that have nothing to do with being genuine and focused when offering praise and worship to God.

At times you may get centered on what you like or what you want from the worship service when you are at church. You may focus on wanting certain songs, specific types of music, or certain instruments. But we have to make sure that we're focused on Jesus and our hearts are pure when giving God praise. We aren't just going through the motions. We're not just there for an experience, but we're desiring a true encounter with God.

Matthew 15:7–8 NLT
"You hypocrites! Isaiah was right when he prophesied about you, for he

wrote, 'These people honor me with their lips, but their hearts are far from me.'"

It is not enough to just show up and sit through a service. Jesus wants more than that: He wants genuine worship from your heart. Our worship to God should go beyond the four walls of the church building. When we're dedicated to live for and worship God, we'll not only worship Him in service but we'll also worship Him with our lifestyle.

Psalms 150:1 KJV
"Praise God in his sanctuary."

We are to lift up the name of Jesus in His sanctuary. This means more than just being in church. It means that any and every time that we are in the presence of God, we have reason to offer Him praise. Every place that we are is a sanctuary because we are never out of the presence of God.

Even outside of the four walls of the church building, you've got to keep praising, praising God's Holy Name. You keep praising even in the hard times, because giving God praise in spite of what you go through will get you all the way through. This is strong faith at work.

Our lifestyle must be marked by the way we press forward, giving God praise continually, and prayer. Praise must be a priority in our lives.!

Praising God will bring you closer to Him. Giving God praise comes naturally out of a thankful heart. When you start your day off by putting God first, praising and worshiping Him for who He is, your day is ordered by the Lord and it goes according to His plan. Disobedience pushes us away from God while obedience brings us closer to God. This is why it's important to keep praising, keep praising God's Holy Name. We're obedient when we give God praise, in spite of what we go through, in spite of what comes our way. When we give God praise it shows that we wholeheartedly depend on Him!

You ought to keep praising God because you know things are about to get better for you. Keep praising God because it's your praise to Him that gets you closer to your destiny. Keep praising God because your faith gets stronger in Him when you continually give God praise. Keep praising God because your praise to God is your weapon against the enemy, against oppression, against spiritual warfare. When you praise God, by faith you become unstoppable, unshakable, untouchable, unchecked, unhindered, and undistracted. Keep praising, because God has given you everything you need to live boldly; to live victoriously; to live a prosperous, abundant, fulfilling, vibrant life in Christ. Keep praising God, because to be focused on our problems is to fear, but to focus on God is to have faith! Giving God praise at all times will help you stay focused.

1 Peter 2:9 KJV
"But ye are a chosen generation, a royal priesthood, an holy nation, a peculiar people; that ye should shew forth the praises of him who hath called you out of darkness into his marvellous light."

Psalm 34:1 KJV
"I will bless the LORD at all times: his praise shall continually be in my mouth."

This first epistle of the Apostle Peter is written to the Hebrew church and to all believers in the body of Christ. He reveals to the reader—you and me—the nature and the identity of the born-again believer in Christ Jesus, those who have their lives devoted to His call and His purposes. In this unique discourse, Peter focuses his gaze on the believer's position in Christ. We are presented with a clear view of what God considers His people to be. Considering this scripture, we must realize who we are today and what we have to do.

The Church finds itself in a time of great power, potential, and possibility. Each day is filled with great opportunities for those who are hungry for an authentic move of God. This is why it's also important to keep praising God. We praise God not only because He created us to; not only to receive so that all of our needs are met; not only because there's purpose in our praise to God; but because we're created to be different, to stand out. We are God's chosen, His Church! We are men and women of vision and power to a hurting world. We are to be devoted. We are to be holy. We are created to be peculiar, giving God all of the praise.

God called us out of darkness into His marvelous light. In 1 Peter 2, God is letting us know that we have been called. Are you willing to accept the challenges that come with your calling?

Ephesians 1:4-5 KJV
"According as he hath chosen us in him before the foundation of the world, that we should be holy and without blame before him in love: Having predestinated us unto the adoption of children by Jesus Christ to himself, according to the good pleasure of his will."

We all have challenges in the world today; they are nothing new. God called us out long ago before the foundation of the world, created and equipped us to not only press through the challenge of tough times but also to be willing to accept the challenge to praise God in spite of tough times. We must show others the goodness of God!

When we remain consistent, and keep praising God, we accept the challenge to stay focused and away from worldly desires. We accept the challenge to live a godly life, being Christ-like, focused on being more like Jesus. It's through our praise that we get the strength we need. It's through our praise that we encourage others in the goodness of the Lord. It's through our praise to God that we get inspired to stay consistent, set the right examples, and set forth the right influence.

We're created to keep praising God because it's through our praise that we become stable. Being stable is a process that takes persistence. Whatever you do, wherever you want to be, whatever you want to accomplish, whatever you go through, you can't fail or lose if you keep at it. This is why we have to keep giving God praise, Family. God wants us to understand the power in being peculiar people. Taking ownership of who God created us to be and how He created us to function, we will always win!

When it comes to being consistent in giving God praise, you cannot be ashamed. Allowing yourself to be ashamed will hold you back from being great, loving what you do, and doing what you love. You must not be ashamed or distracted. You can't let your feelings and emotions control you or get the best of you. Do not yield to temptation but be consistent in your relationship with God, being peculiar and honoring God with the way you live.

Your pressures will turn into praise.

Your doubting will turn into shouting.

Your being depressed will turn into being blessed.

Your misery will turn into ministry.

Your test will turn into a testimony.

Your tragedy will turn into triumph.

Your pain will turn into gain.

Your setback will turn into a comeback.

Your despair will turn into constant prayer.

Your sadness will turn into gladness.

When you're consistent, God will restore the years that you lost in tears.

God will turn your breakdown into breakthrough.

God will turn imprisonment into deliverance!

When you let God have His way, being peculiar with a praise, God turns your situation around for your good! God is changing you from a victim into a victor. God is changing your disaster into destiny. God is changing your persecution into promotion. Family, understand that when the saints (we as God's children) position ourselves to worship God for who He is, in spite of what comes our way, deliverance will take place! When we consistently give God praise, the enemy has no power over us.

Let's keep going, pressing forward in this second chapter, focusing on the importance of praise.

We are to be consistent in the way God created us to live and function in the earth. The word **praise** means "the expression of approval or admiration." The word **admiration** means "someone worthy of respect." Giving God praise is necessary, because we approve and agree that God is who He says He is.

He's worthy of our respect. God has always shown Himself to be faithful, our protector, deliverer, healer, and provider. He is our refuge, our way maker, our miracle worker—all that He declared, He is to us and for us!

Our lives are the evidence: where God brought us from, all that He's done for us, the many times He didn't leave us hanging and didn't allow us to fail. When we were stuck in our own mess, living life the way we wanted to, He preserved us until we came to the point of realizing that enough was enough. He helped us let go of our old ways, waking us to the fact that God's way is the best way. Seeing how good and faithful God has been to us, we have to keep praising, praising God's Holy Name.

This is the importance of giving God praise and being consistent. Because of what we've been through and seeing where we are now, we know that with God it doesn't get any better than this. Can't nobody in this world love us like God can. Can't nobody protect and take care of us like God can. All things work together for our good (Romans 8:28), and life gets better with God—not on our own. We continually give God praise and press forward by faith.

Let's keep going.

Psalm 8:1-9 KJV
"O LORD, our Lord, how excellent is thy name in all the earth! who hast set thy glory above the heavens. Out of the mouth of babes and sucklings hast thou ordained strength because of thine enemies, that thou mightest still the enemy and the avenger. When I consider thy heavens, the work of thy fingers, the moon and the stars, which thou hast ordained; What is man, that thou art mindful of him? and the son of man, that thou visitest him? For thou hast made him a little lower than the angels,

and hast crowned him with glory and honour. Thou madest him to have dominion over the works of thy hands; thou hast put all things under his feet: All sheep and oxen, yea, and the beasts of the field; The fowl of the air, and the fish of the sea, and whatsoever passeth through the paths of the seas. O LORD our Lord, how excellent is thy name in all the earth!"

Life can sometimes seem to go so fast, passing us by. We must be careful and focused, otherwise we will look back one day and wish that we had praised God more.

To praise God is to acknowledge Him: His goodness, holiness, salvation, and grace.

When we find ourselves stuck in tough times, our trouble comes in not finding the time to praise God. When we praise God, we take the focus off of this life and put it onto God.

In Psalm 8, David extols the majesty, power, and providence of God. He praises God's loving-kindness toward mankind, in giving us dominion over this lower world, and the supervision of God, how He covers us. We should praise God just because He deserves praise. There is no other deserving of praise beside God.

Family, it's time to walk in your purpose. It's time to manifest your destiny. It's time to take ownership and be who God has created and called you to be. It's time to be "stedfast, unmoveable, always abounding in the work of the Lord" (1 Corinthians 15:58 KJV). The Lord assigned me to write this book to let you know that the intensity of your struggle is due to the magnitude of your anointing. The Lord will not put more on you that you can bear. If you have a big struggle, that's because God knows you can make it. This is the importance of giving God praise, Family. It doesn't get any better than this!

With God, no matter what comes your way, you can always praise your way through it all in Jesus' Mighty Name.Through your exhortation and through your praise, you can tear down the walls that Satan has built. When you move by faith and give God praise, deliverance takes place and all of Satan's powers are erased. The devil can't touch you when you're in faith giving God praise. I don't care where you go or who you are with, there is no name more excellent than the Lord Jesus!

It doesn't get any better than this!

In Psalm 8, we learn that we as God's children were made a little lower than the angels. We are a royal priesthood and a holy nation. We have the power to overtake anything that comes our way. We are the sons and daughters of God, anointed with authority to change things. Kingdom people should not fear whatever comes their way, because they have the greater One, Jesus, living inside of them.

Praise is what we should do everyday, all day! Praise ought to be a part of our everyday lives. Regardless as to what is going on in our lives, we should not let anything or anybody separate us from or steal the joy we have in Jesus. We serve a mighty God! Because of who He is and all that He's done, doing, and will do, we should be giving God a mighty praise. We have been called to lift up the name of Jesus, to humble ourselves and adore Him.

When we lean on our Almighty God, He will protect and cover us like a fortress. Leaning means to surrender to, depend on, and completely trust in God. When the King of Kings, our Father, is with us, there is nothing that we should fear. In the matchless name of Jesus, the enemy trembles and flees. Any works of the enemy will not come near us in Jesus' Name. God is so good!

This is the importance of praise. This is why we stay consistent and keep praising, keep praising God's Holy Name. Praise and worship is to be our lifestyle. Worship is a way of gladly reflecting back to God the radiance of His worth. We give God praise by keeping our mind stayed on Him and not on difficulties. God is always able, Family, no matter what you are going or will go through. As it always has been, it's time to give God praise! The Bible, God's Word, tells us that God inhabits the praises of his people (Psalm 22:3). It says that we should praise God because we are fearfully and wonderfully made (Psalms 139:14).

Ephesians 6:12 KJV
"For we wrestle not against flesh and blood, but against principalities, against powers, against the rulers of the darkness of this world, against

Although we walk in the flesh, we don't war against the flesh. Our weapons are not of the flesh. Our weapon is our praise! Our praise is used for the destruction of every lofty thing that rises against the knowledge of God.

Let me tell you the story about Paul and Silas in Acts 16. It begins with Paul and Silas locked up in jail. Not only where they locked up, but they were locked up in the innermost cell. Just to make sure they couldn't get out, the guards shackled their feet. The Bible tells us that about midnight, Paul and Silas began to pray and to praise God. Suddenly there was a great earthquake, and the very foundation of the prison began to shake. The prison doors came open, and the shackles became loosed.

When you praise God, doors will begin to open! When you praise God, shackles will begin to loose! If you want to get your deliverance and breakthrough, I am going to tell you what to do: Praise God like it's already happening. Whatever you need, praise God like you already have it. This is how you become consistent and move by faith.

Praise God like the money is already in the bank.

Praise God like your body has already been healed.

Praise God like you already got the promotion.

Praise God like you already have your deliverance.

Praise God like you just got your breakthrough.

Praise God like the strongholds are being lifted.

Praise God like the fire that's shut up in your bones.

Praise God because He's been so good, you can't contain or hold back your praise to Him.

Praise God because He's already won the battle for us.

Praise God because the Lord has given you a garment of praise instead of a spirit of despair.

Praise God because an incredible God deserves an incredible praise.

Praise God because an awesome God deserves an awesome praise.

Keep praising, Family! Keep praising God's Holy Name! When we consistently give God praise, when praises go up, blessings will always come down.

#ByFaithWeGood

CHAPTER 3
KEEP PRAYING!
Keep Praying For Things To Change

Ephesians 6:18 NLT
"Pray in the Spirit at all times and on every occasion. Stay alert and be persistent in your prayers for all believers everywhere."
Praise must be a priority in our lives.

We are to pray without ceasing. Prayer connects us to the power of God, which is necessary to defeat spiritual enemies.

Prayer must become a daily, constant, and consistent way of living. In any given moment, we are only a thought and breath away from communicating with God. Prayer is to permeate believers' lives at all times, with perseverance for all the saints (all of God's children). Praying in the spirit is a form of worship, enabled by the Holy Spirit who intercedes on our behalf. We pray not just for ourselves, but for all saints—all of God's children!

Prayer is one of the biggest assets in a believer's spiritual armory, because with God nothing is impossible.

2 Chronicles 7:14-15 NLT
"Then if my people who are called by my name will humble themselves and pray and seek my face and turn from their wicked ways, I will hear from heaven and will forgive their sins and restore their land. My eyes will be open and my ears attentive to every prayer made in this place."

The Lord is ready and available to help all who call on Him, to hear and answer the prayers of His people. When you take your eyes off Jesus and don't remain prayerful or study God's Word, you can become uncovered. You become distracted and can get caught up under the influence and the power of Satan. You'll find yourself always trying to handle situations on your own. When you take your eyes off Jesus, you'll find yourself in the wrong places at the wrong times.

If prayer is not based on the Word of God, then there is no answer from God.

"Then Jesus said to the disciples, 'Have faith in God. I tell you the truth, you can say to this mountain, 'May you be lifted up and thrown into the sea,' and it will happen. But you must really believe it will happen and have no doubt in your heart. I tell you, you can pray for anything, and if you believe that you've received it, it will be yours.'"

We have to have strong faith and a prayer life to be effective for God. Through prayer, we bring to life what He promised and can function in the way God created us to. There's power in our prayers. When you feel like there's nothing you can do, remember God can!

Prayer is communicating with God for direction. It is casting all your cares on Him because He cares for you (1 Peter 5:7). Prayer empowers you. Prayer keeps your feet in a firm position for what you are believing for God to do in your life. Prayer empowers you to take ownership of who God created you to be. Prayer through faith is a weapon that will destroy your opposition openly.

I say again, there's power in prayer. No matter what the enemy may try, he can't touch our relationship with God. Prayer will destroy the enemy and anything he tries. At the same time, prayer will encourage your heart. Prayer will increase your joy and faith, as you rest in knowing God will always show up for you. Nothing can stop a believer who believes.

1 Corinthians 12:7 NIV
"Now to each one the manifestation of the Spirit is given for the common good."

Romans 8:11 KJV
"But if the Spirit of him that raised up Jesus from the dead dwell in you, he that raised up Christ from the dead shall also quicken your mortal bodies by his Spirit that dwelleth in you."

When you have God's Spirit, you have God's abilities. When you have God's abilities, you can manifest God's Word.

Through prayer with God, you can command what needs to be, whether it's healing, peace, restoration, deliverance, provision, or God's Kingdom. You can speak against everything that has no power: Satan, every demon, every plot, every attack, every scheme and scam, and all sickness. The Greater One lives in you (1 John 4:4), and His name is Jesus!

God's Word and promises do not have an expiration date, and they don't have a closing time. God will listen to us at dusk or dawn, night or day. God will help us no matter what is happening, when it's happening, or who it is happening with. God will send people into our lives—whether it's a loved one, coworker, or even a stranger—to show us that He cares for us.

Psalm 5:2–3 NLT
"Listen to my cry for help, my King and my God, for I pray to no one but you. Listen to my voice in the morning, LORD. Each morning I bring my requests to you and wait expectantly."

Spending time in the morning with God sets the tone of our day. Each day He blesses us with the strength, wisdom, direction and confidence we need to press forward boldly by faith. By faith you can know that God hears you, He's faithful to answer your prayers, you already have guaranteed victory, and everything will work for your good.

Having a prayer life is essential not only to get what you need from God but so you can prepare yourself. Through prayer, you position yourself for God to work on you, removing what needs to be removed, whether it's the worldly way of thinking or having an unforgiving heart. He can remove malice, jealousy, hatred, and insecurities. Removing everything that's not like Him, you prepare yourself through prayer to flow and function in the earth the way God created you to. You can prepare yourself through prayer to be more confident, courageous, focused, and intentional. You are prepared through prayer to go wherever God instructs you to go; you are prepared when God sends you into diverse places and when God intentionally places you among the wicked. He's given you power and authority through Jesus Christ to change what needs to be changed in the world. God said in His Word:

We have to keep praying, praying for things to change, because God has given us power to change things. Nothing should take place in our environments unless we allow it to. There shall be no devil, no demon, no evil forces or spiritual wickedness, no sickness—nothing that is not God's will. Nothing that is against God's will; nothing that will try to block you from walking in the purpose God assigned to your life to fulfill; nothing that will try to block your blessings; nothing that will try to disrupt your peace, joy and happiness has permission to dwell among us. As children of God, we pray because we have the power of God within us to evict from our lives everything the enemy tries to throw at us, in Jesus' Mighty Name!

Family, we have to keep praying, because we're covered when we dwell with God in prayer. We get prepared to live the life God created us to live and to do what God created us to do.

You may ask how to get prepared through prayer. And why? Ask God to reveal His will to you. Prayer is what Jesus did to be in communication with God. Like Him, we must have a heart of obedience and submission to the will of God over our own desires and needs.

We prepare through prayer to prepare for the needs of others.

Remember, it's not about us—it's all about Jesus! Prayer helps you prepare to receive and step into how God wants to use you to meet the needs of others in ministry.

We prepare through prayer to connect with others and other leaders.

We must be around like-minded people and other leaders who are in faith and in the Word of God. They must be doers and not just hearers of the Word of God who will support and motivate you to grow into greatness as the person God created you to be. We must come together to advance God's Kingdom in ministry, in education, in finance, in business, and all over the world.

Pray. Keep praying. We take control of where we are in the way God created us to when we pray constantly. One of the great things about praying is we don't have to be redundant or repetitious in our prayers. God already knows what we have need of before we ask Him (Matthew 6:8). We declare our needs to show God that we acknowledge Him as our only source, that we fully depend on Him.

Our prayers change and become more powerful when we're consistent in our prayer life. The stronger and more consistent we are in prayer, the more God will take care of us. Even more, He'll begin to open our eyes, showing us what and who to pray for. The more we're consistent in prayer, the stronger our discernment will be and the more effectively we'll pray in the Spirit. We will be able to prayerfully tear down strongholds and operate in the anointing God has installed within us to destroy yokes, break curses, cover our families, and be in tune with Him.

Repetition in our prayers is good when we are worshiping God and acknowledging Him for who He is. But redundancy in our prayers can cause us to become stuck and stagnant. It shows lack of faith in God's ability to do what you've requested when we keep asking for the same things that God has already made a way for. That's why God said in Mark 11:24, "Therefore I say unto you, What things soever ye desire, when ye pray, believe that ye receive them, and ye shall have them" (KJV).

Once you pray by faith, it's already happening!

Let's go deeper. Praying and making our requests known to God is like getting in line. Once you pray, you're in line for what you prayed for. Sometimes because of fear, doubt, worry, stress, frustration, and wondering if and when and how, you get out of line to go pray again. You pray for what you've already prayed for just to get back in line when you were already in line.

Family, this is why staying focused is so necessary. It's important to remain in position for what you're believing God to do through you and for you. As children of God, we have a responsibility to get in position, stay in position, and own our position in Christ and with what God has assigned to us. We do this so that God's will is done. We do this so that those that we've been assigned to won't miss out on what God wants to do through us for them. In all things, we give God all the glory.

To avoid being redundant or repetitious in our prayers, we have to understand that what we pray already takes place in the Spirit. It takes strong faith to manifest what we prayed for into the natural realm.

To avoid being redundant or repetitious in our prayers, it is important that we as God's children remain steadfast and patient in our waiting on God. It is easy to feel as though our prayers are not being answered in the time and pace at which we desire. The key thing to remember is that God's timing is the best timing.

Come what may, no matter what your situation looks like, press forward by faith, believing that it's already done. By faith, your situation is already handled and what you need is already in place. God has already worked it out for your good according to His will. Believe by faith that God is with you and has you covered in all areas of your life, and there's nothing the enemy can do about it.

Don't let what you see dictate what you believe. God is so faithful!

In your everyday endeavors, press forward by faith knowing you can accomplish the goals you set out to accomplish. You can be who God says you can be. You can go where God says you can go. You can do what God says you can do. You can have what God says you can have, because there are no limits with God.

The work of waiting often seems to be the most difficult part of our relationship with Jesus Christ, because His timing is different from ours. God doesn't wear a watch, because He's eternal. Yet it only takes a second for Him to show up.

Through prayer, ask God the Father to help you to be patient as you wait on Him. Don't miss out on all God has in store for you because of your own plans or because you're not in faith.

We are not called to be frustrated, stressed out, depressed, and angry.

We were not created to be careless, unloving, jealous, and envious.

God created us by faith so we ought to live by faith.

We ought to set the right examples and put forth the right influences.

We ought to be the light in the dark places. We are the light and the salt in the earth by faith. God created us to show this dying world that Jesus saves, that He's so real and so alive. We lift up the Name of Jesus, so that all others around us will be drawn unto Him!

As you've read, Family, consistent prayer is essential. One way we can also be powerfully effective through prayer is by coming into agreement with each other. When we pray together as a body of believers, there is true power in our agreement.

Our individual prayer lives can be powerful, but we are more powerful when we come together in unity, moving by faith in prayer. We cover each other, our families, children, and friends through prayer, interceding for each other. We go to war together—defeating the enemy and every weapon formed—through prayer. We make sure everyone gets what he or she needs to be strong, healed, focused, and effective through prayer.

Matthew 18:18-20 KJV
"Verily I say unto you, Whatsoever ye shall bind on earth shall be bound in heaven: and whatsoever ye shall loose on earth shall be loosed in heaven. Again I say unto you, That if two of you shall agree on earth as touching anything that they shall ask, it shall be done for them of my Father which is in heaven. For where two or three are gathered together in my name, there am I in the midst of them."

By faith through prayer, we have the power to come together and bind what needs to be bound in the earth: the enemy, every plot or attack, every demon, sickness, depression, anxiety, frustration, doubt, fear, suicidal thoughts, hatred, jealousy, envy, and strife. We have the power to loose what needs to be loosed: God's riches and glory, His promises, peace, joy, love, happiness, respect, unity, prosperity, purpose, fulfillment, success, businesses built on Kingdom principles, God's will being done, and so much more!

When we follow God's Word by faith through prayer, we get results. No matter how tough or difficult situations may seem, when two of us come into agreement for what we pray for, in Jesus' Name it will happen. When two or three of us come together in agreement by faith, God is in the midst of us. We must follow God's instructions and move by faith according to His Word through prayer. Keep praying. Keep praying for things to change!

James 5:15-16 KJV
"And the prayer of faith shall save the sick, and the Lord shall raise him up; and if he have committed sins, they shall be forgiven him. Confess your faults one to another, and pray one for another, that ye may be healed. The effectual fervent prayer of a righteous man availeth much."

There's power in prayer when we pray by faith. Praying by faith produces results, the results of who God is and all that He promised. We must pray with full confidence in God's ability and power to save, heal, deliver, restore, protect, and provide.

In James 5, we see confession and prayer for one another. Through prayer, confession enables us to move forward in the way God created us to. We can let go of our past and the times we've fallen short or made mistakes. We can let go of grudges or how we feel, releasing what needs to be released so that we're functioning by faith and not in fear, guilt, or shame. God is telling us that we're healed when we confess what we've been through and get rid of that which weighs us down, holds us back, and blocks what God wants to do through and for us.

Through prayer we can confess that we are casting all our cares on Jesus because He cares for us (1 Peter 5:7). When you declare this, you deliver yourself from your past, from past hurt, disappointments, let-downs, and mistakes that would hinder you and keep you in your feelings.

Not only can we confess through prayer, but we can come together and help each other. There's power in being in agreement because "the effectual fervent prayer of a righteous man availeth much" (James 5:16 KJV).

1 John 5:14 KJV
"And this is the confidence that we have in him, that, if we ask anything according to his will, he heareth us."

When we pray, we don't pray with uncertainty, we pray with confidence! We have full assurance in Christ Jesus. This is why we keep praying for things to change. A prayer life that flows according to God's will, His way, His plan, His purpose, and His desire will always produce results that are for our good. When we pray according to God's will, we know by faith all will always be well.

You can press forward confidently knowing that God hears you, He's with you, and He has you covered. Praying by faith gives us access to all we have in Christ: Financial increase, guaranteed. Healing, guaranteed. Deliverance, guaranteed. Protection, guaranteed. Restoration, guaranteed. Comfort, guaranteed. Living a purposeful life, guaranteed!

Having said that, God will hear you from anywhere. Daniel prayed in a lion's den. David prayed in a field. Peter prayed on the water and under the water. Jonah prayed from the belly of a great fish. Never let your location or your situation stop you from praying, because God said in His Word to "pray without ceasing" (1 Thessalonians 5:17 KJV). The word ceasing means to bring something to an end.

Family, never stop praying. Praying means we stay in communication with God. We stay tuned into what God is saying, how He's moving, and what's happening around us in the spiritual realm. Rejoice in the Lord always. Pray continually, depending on God at all times.

1 Thessalonians 5:18–19 KJV
"In every thing give thanks: for this is the will of God in Christ Jesus concerning you. Quench not the Spirit."

In other words, give thanks to God in all circumstances, in every situation no matter what your circumstances are. Be thankful and continually give thanks to God, for this is the will of God for you in Christ Jesus. Do not quench—subdue or be unresponsive to the working and guidance of—the Holy Spirit (1 Thessalonians 5:19 KJV). The Holy Spirit is our Counselor who will guide us in our everyday lives. God has given us the Holy Spirit to be our Comforter. He goes before us, removes obstructions, gives us understanding, makes things plain and clear, teaches us all things, shows us what's to come, and leads us in the right direction. The Holy Spirit guides us in all truth so we can differentiate between "okay" choices and the best choices God wants us to make.

We see here, Family, that when we move by faith, we pray continually; we rejoice in the Lord always, giving thanks to God; we submit to the leading of the Holy Spirit; and we do not give up but pray continually. We keep praying, praying for things to change, because by faith all things will change for the better.
Key Points To Remember

We renew our minds through prayer.

We break out of our feelings and move by faith through prayer.

We break out of bad habits and help others (family and friends) break out of bad habits and addictions through prayer.

We bring God's Word alive through prayer.

We change atmospheres through prayer.

We tear down strongholds through prayer.

We get better results in relationships and marriages through prayer.

There's no prayer that God doesn't hear, from a righteous man or woman.

There's no prayer that goes unanswered.

We're created and equipped to pray with strength. God gives us the strength we need to press forward through prayer.

We pray with determination, knowing we shall have what we say. We pray with determination to never give up, never quit. We pray with determination that we will make it in spite of what we're going through or what comes our way, because victory in Jesus is guaranteed. We pray with determination to do the will and work of the Lord. We pray with determination to come out of where we are stronger, wiser, better, ready for greater.

You must also pray with great motivation, because praying with great motivation will break you out of your feelings into "walk[ing] by faith, not by sight" (2 Corinthians 5:7 KJV). You must pray as one motivated by God's love, motivated to stay in communication with Him, motivated to live out what you pray for and declare in Jesus' Name! Get inspired and pray with great motivation, because you've seen what God has done for you before and you know God will do it again. You don't pray as a hobby; you pray because it's your lifestyle and because God is so real and so alive. You choose to function and move by faith and not according to religion or tradition.

Psalm 25:4-5 NLT
"Show me the right path, O LORD; point out the road for me to follow. Lead me by your truth and teach me, for you are the God who saves me. All day long I put my hope in you."

David's prayer expresses his complete trust in God's ability to show him the proper path to take. We read God's Word and seek Him through prayer for knowledge, wisdom, and understanding. Every day that God blesses us to see is an opportunity to put God first and seek Him to lead us, guide us, and teach us in the way we need to go. God's promises are real, and we can be confident that where He leads us in life is always greater than where we've been! We receive guidance and direction for our lives, goals, and what we're truly called to do through the Word of God and by the leading of the Holy Spirit. When you pray by faith and declare the Word of the Lord, you put your trust and hope in Him.

Dear Family, by faith make your requests known to God and thank Him for all the great things He's already done (Philippians 4:6)! By faith, get in position for God to do all that He said He will do. You can rest well and be confident, knowing that God will always show up when you "diligently seek him" (Hebrews 11:6 KJV) through prayer. Keep praying. Keep praying by faith for things to change.

#ByFaithWeGood

BREAKING OUT OF YOUR COMFORT ZONE

Everything That's Comfortable, Ain't Safe

Matthew 25:26-29 NLT
"But the master replied, 'You wicked and lazy servant! If you knew I harvested crops I didn't plant and gathered crops I didn't cultivate, why didn't you deposit my money in the bank? At least I could have gotten some interest on it.' Then he ordered, 'Take the money from this servant, and give it to the one with the ten bags of silver. To those who use well what they are given, even more will be given, and they will have an abundance. But from those who do nothing, even what little they have will be taken away.'"

One of Jesus' most significant parables regarding work is set in the context of investments in Matthew 25. A rich man delegates the management of his wealth to his servants, much like investors in today's markets. He gives five talents (a large unit of money) to the first servant, two talents to the second, and one talent to the third. Two of the servants earn one hundred percent returns by trading with the funds, but the third servant hides the money in the ground and earns nothing. The rich man returns and rewards the two who made money but severely punishes the servant who did nothing.

The meaning of the parable reaches far beyond financial investments. God has given each person a wide variety of gifts, and he expects us to employ those gifts in His service. It is not acceptable to merely put those gifts on a closet shelf and ignore them. Like the three servants, we do not have gifts of the same degree. The return God expects of us is commensurate with the gifts we have been given. The servant who received one talent was not condemned for failing to reach the five-talent goal; he was condemned because he did nothing with what he was given. The gifts we receive from God include skills, abilities, family connections, social positions, education, experiences, and more.

The point of the parable is that we are to use whatever we have been given for God's purposes. The severe consequences to the unproductive servant tell us that we are to invest our lives, not waste them.

God doesn't want you to always dwell in your comfort zone. What are you doing with what you have? You have prosperity in your hands! When you identify whose you are—a child of God—and what you carry, you can fulfill your purpose. When we understand the value of what God has given us, we will want to give it all back to Him and thensome.

God wants to work with what you have. We cannot neglect what God gave us. If we are not productive, God will raise up someone else who is. We won't reap the benefits He promised in this life and eternally because we didn't put in the work.

Your comfort zone is not a safe place. Comfort zones can become sinking sand when you allow fear to come in and tell you that you can't go any further. Fear is a lie! God equips us for where He's leading us and how He wants to use us. No matter what you may go through, come what may, even when God moves "Suddenly"—He is never too late. God can and God will restore. Imagine how much God can do to restore your years, to give you back what you lost, and to reward you for waiting patiently on His promises.

Know that "Suddenly" moments aren't limited by time, "for we walk by faith, not by sight" (2 Corinthians 5:7 KJV).

Get ready for your "suddenly" moment!

Sometimes it seems like you've stepped out on faith, but now you're out on a limb. You believe God, but your circumstances aren't giving you reasons to confidently trust Him. The desires of your heart are starting to feel more like dreams than promises. Remember, Family, God specializes in providing right on time. You can believe what God says because "God is not a man that He should lie" (Numbers 23:19 KJV). God can't lie! God is so invested in you that He numbered the hairs on your head (Luke 12:7). God has a master plan and will never leave you out on a limb without making a way for you to come back to solid ground.

Don't let fear rob you of your destiny. Submit your gifts to God and allow Christ to use you. Submit every area of your heart to Christ and let God lead and light your path. To be who God has called us to be, we must have faith and take decisive action. It may be scary at first, but we can have peace knowing that when we seek God, He will not fail us.

Family, everything that's comfortable ain't safe!

As humans, we always want to be comfortable. We love to be comfortable. I know this to be true for myself. A lot of us hate discomfort, but I have learned in my own life that I always perform best when I am uncomfortable. Moving to new locations, attending new schools, and starting new jobs usually produce some of the best results in our lives.

Whether in the realm of academia or relationships, comfort is bad business. For example, when pursuing a romantic relationship, people will go the extra mile to wow the other individual. However, the moment that they feel they've successfully wowed their partner, comfort kicks in and the relationship can grow cold.

The problem is that humans, even children of God, love to get comfortable. We get too content to change and grow as we should.

That couple I mentioned above may become exasperated, because they are not truly caring about each other. How then do you think God feels when we're so comfortable that we act like we don't care about or love Him? How do you think God feels when we are going through tough times and question whether or not we should even follow Him, because "It's too hard, it's too uncomfortable, and I don't feel like it"? How do you think He feels when we tell Him we no longer have to bind and rebuke that spirit of comfort because we are done with "doing that"?

The Bible tells us that Satan comes to tempt us and draw us away from God during difficult seasons—especially seasons that bring us to a crossroads of choosing whether to believe in God or simply forget Him. Satan will tell us we don't need Christ and try to make us feel as if we are invincible, yet Christ is the one who has delivered us from countless forms of bondage. Satan will try to convince us that we are humble when we are instead being arrogant and losing our respect for God, His ways, and His rules.

You must never stop praising God and submitting to His will. Faith even as small as a mustard seed (Matthew 17:20) and obedience to God will move you to the next level in Him. You may not be satisfied with where you are in life, but you can be satisfied with Jesus. Break out of where you are with what God has given you. Always look to move forward, to do greater things. We must be ready at all times to follow God (Matthew 16:24), because the best is still yet to come.

God's got a blessing with your name on it. God is saying to you, "It's time to stop sitting around and waiting for something to happen." It's time that you start living like you belong to God. You can press forward by faith and possess what God has for you. All you have to do is move.

Everything that's comfortable ain't safe!

How many of us have been in hiding? How many of us stay away from the forefront and bury the testimonies that God has given us because we don't feel like sharing? Are we so concerned with people accepting who we are that we hide who God has made us to be?

Family, never be afraid to share what God has done for you. You must share where God has brought you from, where He has you now, and where you're pressing toward as He leads you by faith. We share our testimonies to give God glory. Our testimonies honor God and help others who may be going through the same difficulties, tough circumstances, struggles, trials, and tribulations we went through. By sharing, we encourage them to trust that what God did for us, He'll do for them too.

Never be ashamed of who you are and what you've been through. We are blessed to tell others what we have been through, because these are our stories, our testimonies. It doesn't matter what people say or if they judge you. What we've been through has made us stronger, wiser, and more focused. We are ready for all that God has in store for us, and, most importantly, we are ready for all that God wants to do through us. We add value to this world by helping others, advancing God's Kingdom, and giving God all the glory.

Everything that's comfortable ain't safe!

2 Corinthians 1:3–5 NLT
"All praise to God, the Father of our Lord Jesus Christ. God is our merciful Father and the source of all comfort. He comforts us in all our troubles so that we can comfort others. When they are troubled, we will be able to give them the same comfort God has given us. For the more we suffer for Christ, the more God will shower us with his comfort through Christ."

We do not need to fear discomfort, because God will always give us the comfort we need, especially in times of trouble. No matter what obstacles or challenges may come our way, we can get uncomfortable because the God of all comfort covers us when we need Him.

Paul opens his second letter to the Corinthians by praising a God who gives so much mercy and comfort to the apostle and all believers. We get the impression that Paul knows the mercy and comfort of God firsthand. Family, we can learn from Paul's example: though he was called to be uncomfortable at times, he never worried about what would happen or if he'd make it. Like Paul, by faith we can go where God says go, do what God created us to do, and be who God created us to be!

God's Word encourages us to "come boldly unto the throne of grace, that we may obtain mercy, and find grace to help in time of need" (Hebrews 4:16 KJV). The Lord is able to give peace to the troubled conscience and to calm the raging passions of the soul. He gives these blessings as the Father of His redeemed family.

Our Savior Jesus Christ says, "let not your heart be troubled" (John 14:1 KJV), for all comfort comes from God. Our sweetest comforts are in Him. He speaks peace to souls by granting the free remission of sins, and He comforts all by the enlivening influences of the Holy Spirit and the rich mercies of His grace. He is able to bind up the broken-hearted, to heal the most painful wounds, and to give hope and joy under the heaviest sorrows. The favor God bestows on us not only makes us whole and cheerful but also useful to Him and others.

We can get uncomfortable because God sends the perfect comfort to support those who simply trust and serve Him. If we should be brought so low as to despair of life, even then may we trust God, who can bring reverse death. Our hope and trust in God is not in vain, nor shall any be ashamed who trust in the Lord.

Past experiences encourage faith and hope and lay us under obligation to trust in God for times to come. It is our duty to help one another through prayer, in praise and thanksgiving, as we press forward thereby making suitable returns for benefits received, producing good fruit in the earth. By faith, both trials and mercies will end in good for ourselves and others!

You may wonder why God has allowed certain difficulties into your life. Instead of asking why, ask Him to comfort you. The only comfort you should seek is comfort from God. He comforts us in our troubles so that we can, in turn, comfort others. Think about it. It's the people who've been through pain like our own who can comfort us when we are hurting.

What hard times has God allowed you to go through? Family problems? A problem at school or at your job? Have you struggled with low self-esteem or a poor self-image?

As you press forward by faith, and resist becoming too comfortable, know that you can always get comfort and strength from God. He may enable you to comfort someone in a similar situation. Press on, seeking God as the only source of comfort on which you can depend.

Psalm 121:1-2 KJV
"I will lift up mine eyes unto the hills, from whence cometh my help. My help cometh from the LORD, which made heaven and earth."

Family, it is time to change your mindset. Let the Lord use you to show love towards others. Build up your confidence in the Lord and press forward by faith. What has He laid on your heart to do? I encourage you to do it! Start your business, enroll in the school, apply for that job, start writing your book, begin that project, work toward accomplishing the goals you set, branch out of your comfort zone and start networking with new people. Go where God says go, and do what He says to do. God is with you. He will give you the knowledge, wisdom, strength, and ability to do what He called you to.

Romans 12:2 KJV
"And be not conformed to this world: but be ye transformed by the renewing of your mind, that ye may prove what is that good, and acceptable, and perfect, will of God."

Some of us are too comfortable in this world. We need to rise up and have a stronger desire for God: who He is, His will, His way, His plan, His purpose, and His desire. We must seek what God wants more than what we want. Family, you must give God praise; be consistent in what God has called and created you to do; and have Jesus Christ as your Lord and Savior. This can save your life and position you to experience the greater days He has in store for you. It is time to experience the "goodness of the Lord in the land of the living" (Psalms 27:13).

Jesus got uncomfortable when He came into the world to show us the way. He got uncomfortable to be our example of how to live in the way He created us to. Jesus got uncomfortable when He allowed Himself to get arrested and taken through a mock trial. He got uncomfortable when He allowed Himself to be sentenced to death and whipped. Jesus got uncomfortable when He humbled Himself and carried the cross to Calvary. Jesus got uncomfortable when He allowed the Roman soldiers to nail Him to the cross. He got uncomfortable and allowed them to lift Him up, so He could draw all men unto Himself (John 12:32). Jesus got uncomfortable when He shed His blood for us, gave up His spirit, and hung His head and died.

But because Jesus got uncomfortable, three days later, He got up with all power in His hands! God loves us so much that He sent

Jesus to get uncomfortable enough to save us and set us free.

Because Jesus got uncomfortable, we ought to get uncomfortable. Like Jesus, we must remember that with God we never lose. We never fail, but we always win. Family, press forward and move by faith. Be great. Be fearless. Shine bright!

With God, we always win. Get uncomfortable, because everything that's comfortable ain't safe!

#ByFaithWeGood!

To God Be All The Glory!

TESTIMONY

Hey Family.

Can I be transparent and share our testimony that will encourage you to never give up?

My wife Vanessa and I moved into our new house in December 2020. It was a new build. Originally we were scheduled to close on November 20th, 2020, but due to complications with the underwriter, our closing day was postponed.

Underwriters are responsible for deciding whether or not to accept and approve applications, and this one underwriter really gave us a hard way to go. She constantly kept throwing stuff at us that we needed to do before we closed. Every time we got to the point of closing, she would say, "Well, you have to do this," or "Now you gotta do that," or "Now you have to make sure of this." I mean, every time we got to the point of closing, she found more stuff we needed to do!

Finally, we did all that was asked of us. We were all ready to schedule our closing, when the underwriter told me and my wife that there was one more thing. In order to close, we needed to be making a certain additional amount of money on top of our current salaries, and that amount needed to include a bonus.

At this point, frustration came into play. My wife was ready to let it go and be done with the whole situation. I told her, "No, everything this underwriter throws at us, we'll accomplish. She can't block what God ordained for us to have."

Because I had just gotten a promotion, I couldn't request any additional money. My wife had to go to her job. I told her she has the favor of God on her life: Walk in it and ask her for the raise. She asked her boss, and her boss immediately approved the increase, as well as the bonus!

A week later, we received an email that we were cleared to close!

This underwriter tried everything she could to block us, but we didn't back down. Because we were praying, trusting God's Word, and walking by faith, she had to bow down and give us what was ours in Jesus' Name.

Family, we want to encourage you to never give up. No thing and no one can block where God has ordained you to be and what God has ordained for you to have. No matter what comes your way, God has equipped you to handle it all. You can overcome every obstacle and press through every challenge!

Every time this underwriter threw something at us, we knocked it out and got it done. Family, never give up. With God, you'll always win!

**#MoveByFaith #PressForward #WithGodYouAreCovered
#ByFaithWeGood #ToGodBeAllTheGlory!**

IT'S YOUR TIME

"Extending The Invitation"

Romans 10:9 KJV
"That if thou shalt confess with thy mouth the Lord Jesus, and shalt believe in thine heart that God hath raised him from the dead, thou shalt be saved."

As you've been reading this book, perhaps these words have spoken to you in a special way. With all that you've read, you now want to receive and experience who God is for yourself. You want to position yourself to "[cast] all your care upon him; for he careth for you" (1 Peter 5:7 KJV).

I encourage to accept Jesus Christ into your life as your Lord and Savior. Falling in love with Jesus is the best thing that has ever happened to me. When you accept Christ into your life, you'll also be a witness that falling in love with Jesus is the best thing that's ever happened to you! God freely adopts us into His eternal family. I encourage you to open up your heart today, and invite Jesus into your life and into all of your circumstances.

If the person I'm speaking to is you, repeat this prayer:

Father, forgive me, for I have sinned and fallen short of Your glory.
I believe that Jesus Christ is the Son of God.
I believe that Jesus Christ died for my sins.
I believe that Jesus Christ rose with all power.
I believe that Jesus Christ is so real and so alive.
Jesus, save me. I accept you as my Lord and Savior. Come into my heart. Come into my life, and stay in my life.
Holy Spirit, come into my heart. Come into my life and stay in my life. Have your way, so that I live according to God's Word, His will, and His way.
In Jesus' Name, Amen!

Family, if you fully believe in the prayer you just declared, you just got saved! This day will be the start and new beginning of the best days of the rest of your life.

Your time for greater is now. Stay focused, and always press forward by faith!

#ByFaithWeGood

CONCLUSION

Family, thank you so much for your support and for taking the time to read this book. I pray that you are inspired and encouraged to be consistent in the way God created you to live and function in the earth, always pressing forward by faith!

I'm forever grateful for how God used me to lift Him up and to encourage and pray for you all throughout this book. It is all for His glory! I pray that every word has truly been a blessing to you. As you press forward, I will continue to encourage and pray for you as God allows. It is not about us, but it is and always will be all about Jesus. His will. His way. His plan. His purpose. His desire. Let us seek what God wants more than what we want, looking forward to all that God is going to do through and for us in the years to come.

Ephesians 3:17-19 KJV
"That Christ may dwell in your hearts by faith; that ye, being rooted and grounded in love, May be able to comprehend with all saints what is the breadth, and length, and depth, and height; And to know the love of Christ, which passeth knowledge, that ye might be filled with all the fullness of God."

I pray that out of God's glorious riches He will strengthen you with power through His Spirit in your inner being, so that Christ may dwell in your hearts through faith. I pray that you, being rooted and established in love, may have power, together with all the Lord's holy people, to grasp how wide and long and high and deep the love of Christ is. I pray that you may know God's love that surpasses knowledge—that you may be filled to the measure of all the fullness of God.

God is always with you.

He'll always have you covered.

God is always able.

Things are about to get better for you in Jesus' Mighty Name.

Let Jesus lead you.

Stay focused and always press forward by faith!

#ByFaithWeGood

ABOUT THE AUTHOR

Minister Bernard Marrow is a native of Philadelphia, Pennsylvania. Currently living in the State of Illinois, he is the founder and president of ByFaithWeGood – BFWGMinistry.

Minister Bernard Marrow is a singer, songwriter, and musician. He is a faithful, dedicated, hard worker who was ordained as a Deacon on June 18th, 2011, received his ministerial license on April 27th, 2014 under the leadership of Pastor Robert T. Moore Jr. He currently resides in Chicago, Illinois with his beautiful wife, Vanessa where he was relicensed as a minister at Empowered People Church a ministry under Kingdom Church International Ministries on January 9th, 2022 under the leadership of Pastors Drs. John & Kisia Coleman Overseer & Lead Pastor.

With the release of his second book The 3 P's, through the leading of the Holy Spirit, Minister Bernard has provided a resource for believers to use every day to help them stay focused and grounded in who God is and His Word. He encourages believers to always press forward by faith. Minister Bernard Marrow is a man of prayer, very passionate about the purpose God assigned to his life. He focuses on equipping others to be strong in their faith, always grounded in God's Word and advancing God's Kingdom!

Why? Because **ByFaithWeGood!**

"For We Walk By Faith, Not By Sight"
2 Corinthians 5:7 KJV

CONNECT WITH THE AUTHOR

Minister Bernard On Facebook: **Min Bernard Marrow**
ByFaithWeGood on Facebook: **By Faith We Good Ministry Inc.**

Instagram: **@min.marrow**
ByFaithWeGood Instagram: **@bfwgministry**

Snapchat: **Min. Marrow**

Twitter: **@MinMarrow**
ByFaithWeGood: **@ByFaithWeGood**

Email:
Min. Bernard Marrow:
connectwithmin.marrow@gmail.com

ByFaithWeGood:
info@bfwgministry.com

Websites:
www.BFWGMinistry.com
www.ShopBFWG.com